BULLETPOINTS

GREEKS & ROMANS

John Farndon
Consultant: Steve Parker

Miles Kelly
PUBLISHING

First published in 2003 by Miles Kelly Publishing Ltd
Bardfield Centre, Great Bardfield
Essex, CM7 4SL

2 4 6 8 10 9 7 5 3 1

Project Manager: Ruthie Boardman

Design: Venita Kidwai

Picture Research: Liberty Newton

Assistant: Carol Danenbergs

Production: Estela Godoy

British Library Cataloguing-in-Publication Data
A catalogue record for this book is available from the British Library

ISBN 1-84236-259-3

Printed in China

www.mileskelly.net
info@mileskelly.net

The publishers would like to thank the following artists who have contributed to this book:
Richard Berridge, Venessa Card, Nicholas Forder, Chris Forsey, Mike Foster, Terry Gabbey
Richard Hook, John James, Roger Kent, Aziz Khan, Kevin Maddison, Janos Marffy, Roger Payne,
Terry Riley, Martin Sanders, Rob Sheffield, Peter Sarson, Guy Smith, Roger Stewart,
Studio Galante, Mike Taylor, Rudi Vizi, Mike White, John Woodcock

All other images are from: MKP archives; Corel

Contents

Ancient Crete

- **The Minoan** civilization of Crete – an island south of Greece – was the first civilization in Europe.

- **Minoan** civilization began about 3000BC, reached its height from 2200 to 1450BC, then mysteriously vanished – perhaps after the volcano on nearby Santorini erupted.

- **The name** *Minoan* comes from the Greek legend of King Minos. Minos was the son of Europa, the princess seduced by the god Zeus in the shape of a bull.

- **Greek stories** tell how Minos built a labyrinth (maze) in which he kept the Minotaur, a monster with a man's body and a bull's head.

- **Catching a bull** by the horns and leaping over it (bull-leaping) was an important Minoan religious rite.

- **Experts** now think Minos was a title, so every Cretan king was called Minos.

- **The Minoans** were great seafarers and traded all over the eastern Mediterranean.

- **At the centre** of each Minoan town was a palace, such as those found at Knossos, Zakro, Phaestos and Mallia.

▲ *The minotaur of Greek myth.*

- **The largest** Minoan palace is at Knossos. It covered 20,000 square metres and housed over 30,000 people.

- **The walls** of the palace are decorated with frescoes (paintings), which reveal a great deal about the Minoans.

▼ *The famous Minoan palace at Knossos*

The Trojan Wars

- **From 1600 to 1100BC,** mainland Greece was dominated by tough warrior people called the Mycenaeans.

- **The Mycenaeans** fought with long bronze swords, long leather shields and bronze armour.

- **Mycenaeans** lived in small kingdoms, each with its own fortified hilltop city – called an *acropolis*.

- **A typical** Mycenaean noble was like a Viking chieftain. In the middle of his palace was a great hall with a central fireplace where warriors would sit around, telling tales of heroic deeds.

- **After 1500BC,** Mycenaean kings were buried in a beehive-shaped tomb called a *tholos*, with a long, corridor-shaped entrance.

- **The Greek poet** Homer tells how a city called Troy was destroyed by the Mycenaeans after a 10-year siege. Historians once thought this was just a story, but now that Troy's remains have been discovered, they think there may be some truth in it.

▶ *Troy fell when the Greeks pretended to give up and go home, leaving behind a huge wooden horse. The jubilant Trojans dragged this into the city – only to discover Greeks hiding inside it.*

▶ *The Trojan War lasted for ten bloody years. Many lives were lost during battles, even though the soldiers wore protective armour. Achilles and Hector would have worn crested helmets like those shown here, to make them look more frightening and impressive. A bronze breast plate would have protected the upper body while bronze leg guards were worn to protect the lower legs.*

- **The Trojan War** in Homer's tale is caused by the beautiful Helen of Sparta. She married Menalaus, brother of King Agamemnon of Mycenae, but she fell in love with Prince Paris of Troy.

- **Helen and Paris** eloped to Troy and Agamemnon and other Greeks laid siege to Troy to take her back.

- **The battle** featured many heroes – such as Hector, Achilles and Odysseus.

- **The Greeks** finally captured Troy when Greek soldiers hidden inside a wooden horse found their way into the city.

Early Greece

- **Around 1200BC,** the Mycenaeans began to abandon their cities, and a people called the Dorians took over Greece.

- **Many Mycenaeans** fled overseas in a large battle fleet, and the Egyptians called them the Sea Peoples. Some ended up in Italy and may have been the ancestors of the Etruscan people there.

- **With the end** of Mycenaean civilization, Greece entered its Dark Ages as the art of writing was lost.

- **About 800BC,** the Greeks began to emerge from their Dark Ages as they relearned writing from the Phoenicians, a people who traded in the eastern Mediterranean.

- **The period** of Greek history from 800–500BC is called the Archaic (Ancient) Period.

- **In the Archaic** Period, the Greek population grew rapidly. States were governed by rich aristocrats.

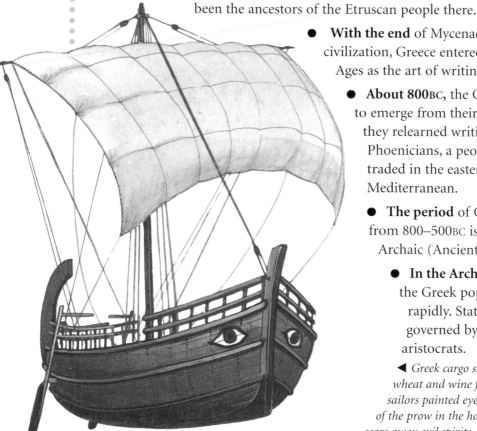

◄ *Greek cargo ships carried oil, wheat and wine for trading. The sailors painted eyes on either side of the prow in the hope they would scare away evil spirits.*

8

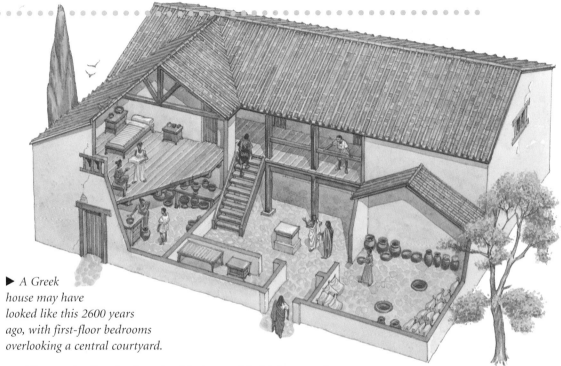

▶ *A Greek
house may have
looked like this 2600 years
ago, with first-floor bedrooms
overlooking a central courtyard.*

- **The early Greeks** loved athletics and held four major
  events. They were called the Panhellenic Games and drew competitors
  from all over the Greek world.

- **The four** Panhellenic Games were the Olympic, Pythian, Isthmian and
  Nemean Games.

- **The Olympic Games** started in 776BC and were the most important.
  They were held every four years, at Olympia.

- **The Greek poet** Homer wrote his famous poems about the Trojan Wars
  around 700BC

Greek city-states

- **Ancient Greece** was not a single country in its early days, but a collection of independent cities or city-states.

- **A Greek city-state** was called a *polis* (plural *poleis*).

- *Polis* gives us the words politics and police – and polite.

- **There were** several hundred poleis in ancient Greece. The largest were Athens and Sparta.

- **Each city** typically had a mound called an *acropolis* with a temple on top, and a market place called an *agora*.

- **To start with** (from about 800–600BC), city-states were governed by oligarchs (a few powerful men) or a tyrant, but other people gradually got more say in how things were run.

- **People in Greek city-states** were either free or slaves. Free men (not women) were split into citizens (born in the city itself) and *metics* (immigrants).

- **In 508BC,** a man called Cleisthenes gave Athens a new system of government called democracy.

- **Democracy** comes from the Greek word *demos* ('people') and *kratos* ('rule'). The idea was that every citizen (except metics and slaves) had the right to speak and vote in the Assembly, held every ten days on a hill called the Pnyx.

▼ *The most famous acropolis is the Acropolis in Athens with the Parthenon temple on top, but nearly every polis (city-state) had one.*

··· **FASCINATING FACT** ···
The laws of the Athenian oligarch Draco were so harsh that severe laws are still called 'draconian'.

Greek thinkers

▲ *Euclid, great Greek mathematician and author of the 13-volume work,* Elements, *was teaching in Alexandria around 300BC.*

- **The great** thinkers of ancient Greece were called philosophers. *Philosophy* is Greek for 'love of wisdom'.

  - **The key** philosophers were Socrates, Plato and Aristotle.

    - **Socrates** (466–399BC) believed people would behave well if they knew what good behaviour was and challenged people to think about truth, good and evil.

    - **Plato** (427–348BC) argued that, behind the messy chaos of everyday experience, there is a perfect and beautiful Idea or Form. He also tried to find the ideal way of governing a state.

  - **Aristotle** (384–322BC) argued that, for true knowledge, you must find the 'final cause' – why something happens.

  - **Aristotle** was the first great scientist, stressing the need to collect data, sort the results and interpret them.

- **Many of** the basic ideas in philosophy, even today, come from Socrates, Plato and Aristotle, and other Greek philosophers such as Epicurus and Diogenes.

- **Greek mathematicians** such as Euclid, Appolonius, Pythagoras and Archimedes worked out many of our basic rules of maths. Most school geometry still depends on the system devised by Euclid.

- **Greek astronomers** like Aristarchus and Anaxagoras made many brilliant deductions – but many of these were forgotten. Aristarchus realized that the Earth turned on its axis and circled the Sun. Yet it was almost 2000 years before this idea was generally accepted.

▲ Aristotle, the brilliant tutor to Alexander the Great, was thought of as the ultimate authority on every subject for over 2000 years.

> ...FASCINATING FACT...
> Archimedes showed how the effect of a lever could be worked out by maths.

Greek art

- **In the heyday** of ancient Greece, thousands of sculptors, architects, painters, dramatists and poets were creating a fantastic wealth of beautiful works of art.

- **The Greeks** made graceful statues and friezes to decorate temples and homes. They were carved mostly from marble and limestone and then painted, though in surviving statues the paint has worn away.

- **The most famous** sculptors were Phidias (*c.*490–420BC), Praxiteles (*c.*330BC), Lysippus (*c.*380–306BC) and Myron (*c.*500–440BC). Phidias's huge gold and ivory statue of the god Zeus was famed throughout the ancient world.

- **Greek architects** such as Ictinus and Callicrates created beautiful marble and limestone temples fronted by graceful columns and elegant triangular friezes. The most famous is the Parthenon in Athens.

- **The Greeks** had three styles for columns: the simple Doric, the slender Ionic, topped by scrolls, and the ornate Corinthian, topped by sculpted acanthus leaves.

- **The style** created by the Greek temples is now called Classical and has influenced architects ever since.

- **The Greeks** believed that different arts (such as dance or poetry) were inspired by one of nine goddesses, who were known as the Muses.

- **Ancient Greek** writers include the poets Homer, Sappho and Pindar. They created styles of writing that included epic poetry – long, dramatic tales of heroic deeds.

▲ *The famous Venus de Milo was found on the Aegean island of Milos in AD1820. It was carved in Greek Antioch (now in Turkey) around 150BC and shows the goddess of love, Aphrodite (Roman goddess Venus). The statue originally had arms.*

- **The tragedy** is a grand drama doomed to end unhappily for the hero. Tragedy was created by Greek dramatists such as Aeschylus, Euripides and Sophocles, who wrote the tragedy *King Oedipus*.

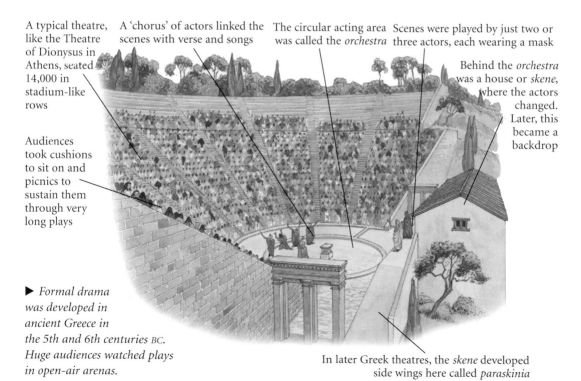

A typical theatre, like the Theatre of Dionysus in Athens, seated 14,000 in stadium-like rows

A 'chorus' of actors linked the scenes with verse and songs

The circular acting area was called the *orchestra*

Scenes were played by just two or three actors, each wearing a mask

Behind the *orchestra* was a house or *skene*, where the actors changed. Later, this became a backdrop

Audiences took cushions to sit on and picnics to sustain them through very long plays

▶ *Formal drama was developed in ancient Greece in the 5th and 6th centuries BC. Huge audiences watched plays in open-air arenas.*

In later Greek theatres, the *skene* developed side wings here called *paraskinia*

15

Greek mythology

- **The Greeks had a** wealth of myths – stories about their gods, goddesses, heroes and villains.

- **We know about** the myths mainly from Homer's poems and Hesiod's book *Theogeny*, both from about 700BC.

- *Theogeny* tells how the Earth began, with the earth goddess Gaia emerging from chaos and giving birth to Uranus, the king of the sky.

- **The many children** of Gaia and Uranus were called the Titans, led by Cronos.

- **Cronos married** his sister Rhea. Their children, led by Zeus, rebelled against the Titans to become the new top gods, called the Olympians.

- **The Olympians** were said to live on Mount Olympus, and include the most famous Greek gods, such as Apollo the god of light, Demeter the goddess of crops, Artemis the goddess of the Moon and Dionysius the wine god.

◀ ▲ *Many Greek gods were adopted by the Romans. The winged messenger Hermes (above) became Mercury in ancient Rome, while Aphrodite, the goddess of love (left), became Venus.*

- **Greek heroes** were mostly those who had performed great deeds during the times of the Trojan Wars or earlier.

- **Early heroes** include Jason, who led his Argonauts (his crew) in search of the fabulous Golden Fleece, and Theseus, who killed the Minotaur.

- **Trojan war** heroes included Achilles and Odysseus.

- **The greatest hero** was super-strong Heracles, whom the Romans would later call Hercules.

▶ *King of the Greek gods was Zeus. He ruled from his home on Mount Olympus and headed a group of Greek gods called the Olympians. Zeus is a weather and sky god and is especially associated with thunder and lightning. The Roman god Jupiter is the equivalent to Zeus.*

17

Homer

- **Homer** is the ancient Greek poet said to have written the ancient world's two greatest poems: the *Iliad* and the *Odyssey*.

- **Homer** probably lived in the 9th century BC in Ionia, on what is now the Aegean coast of Turkey, or on the island of Chios.

- **No one** knows for certain if Homer actually existed, or if he composed all of both poems. Most current experts think that he did.

- **In Homer's time** there was a great tradition of bards. These were poets who recited aloud great tales of heroic deeds. They knew the poems by heart and so never wrote them down.

- **The *Iliad*** and the *Odyssey* are the only poems from the times of the bards that were written down and so survive. They may have been written down at the time, or later.

- **After Homer's time,** the two great poems were used in religious festivals in Greece.

- **For centuries** after Homer's time, Greek children learned to read, and learned about the legends of the past, by studying Homer's two great poems.

- **In the 2nd century BC,** scholars at the Alexandrian Library in Egypt studied the poems. A few scholars came to the conclusion that they were so different in style they must have been written by two different poets.

▲ *Nothing is known for certain about Homer, but legend says that he was blind.*

- The *Iliad* is a long poem in lofty language about the Trojan Wars, in which the Greeks besiege the city of Troy to take back the kidnapped Helen.

- The *Odyssey* tells of a great journey made by hero Odysseus, and his adventures along the way.

▶ *The* Odyssey *recounts the adventures of Odysseus on his 10-year journey home after the war against Troy. In one tragic scene, Odysseus's faithful old dog Argus dies as his master reaches his home town.*

19

Alexander the Great

- **Alexander the Great** was a young Macedonian king who was one of the greatest generals in history. He built an empire stretching from Greece to India.

- **Alexander was born** in 356BC in Pella, capital of Macedonia. His father, King Phillip II, was a tough fighter who conquered neighbouring Greece. His mother was the fiery Olympias, who told him that he was descended from Achilles, the hero of the *Iliad*.

Alexander the Great

- **As a boy,** he was tutored by the famous philosopher Aristotle. A story tells how he tamed the unridable ho Bucephalus, which afterwards carried him as far as India.

- **When Alexander** was 20, his father was murdered by a bodyguard and he became king. Alexander quickly stamped out rebellion.

- **In 334BC,** Alexander crossed the narrow neck of sea separating Europe from Asia with his army. Within a year, he had conquered the mighty Persian Empire.

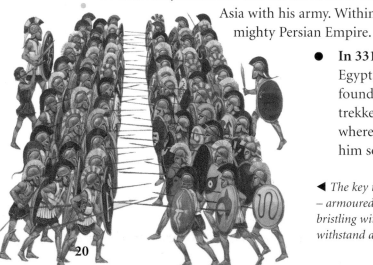

- **In 331BC,** Alexander led his army into Egypt, where he was made pharaoh and founded the city of Alexandria. He trekked to the desert oasis of Siwah, where legend says an oracle proclaimed him son of the Greek god Zeus.

◀ *The key to Macedonian success was the phalanx – armoured soldiers standing in tightly packed rows bristling with long spears. Such a formation could withstand a cavalry attack, yet still move swiftly.*

- **In 327BC,** he married the lovely Bactrian princess, Roxane.

- **After capturing** the city of Babylon and finishing off the Persian king, Darius, Alexander led his conquering army into India. Here his homesick troops finally asked to go home.

> **FASCINATING FACT**
> An old legend said that anyone who untied a tricky knot in a town called Gordium would conquer Asia. Alexander instantly sliced through this Gordian knot with his sword.

- **In 325BC,** Alexander had ships built and carried his army down the Indus River and returned to Babylon. Within a year, he fell ill and died.

▶ *In just nine years and a series of brilliant campaigns, Alexander created a vast empire. No one knows exactly what his plans were. However, the teachings of his tutor Aristotle were important to him, and he had his own vision of different peoples living together in friendship.*

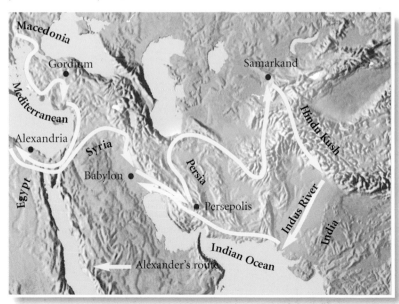

21

The birth of Rome

- **People were living** in Italy long before Rome was founded and a people called the Etruscans created an advanced civilization in the northwest between 800 and 400BC.

- **According to legend,** Rome was founded in 753BC by the twins Romulus and Remus, who were said to have been brought up by a she-wolf.

- **By 550BC,** Rome was a big city ruled by Etruscan kings.

- **In 509BC,** the Roman people drove out the kings and formed themselves into an independent republic.

▲ *Senators were men from leading citizen families who had served the Roman republic as judges or state officials. They made new laws and discussed government plans.*

▲ *The first rules of the Roman legal system were recorded in 450BC in a document called the* Twelve Tables. *The Roman system forms the basis of many legal systems today.*

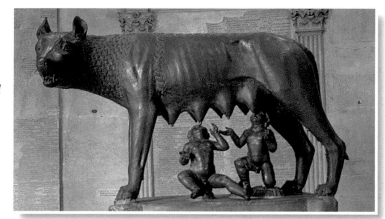

▶ *Legend has it that after founding the city of Rome, Romulus and Remus quarrelled and Romulus killed his brother.*

- **Republican Rome** was ruled by the Senate, an assembly made up of 100 patricians (men from leading families).

- **In theory,** Rome was governed by the people. However, real power was in the hands of patricians; plebeians (ordinary citizens) had little. Slaves had no power or rights at all.

- **Plebeians fought** for power and, by 287BC, gained the right to stand as consuls, the highest official posts.

- **In the 400s** and 300s BC, Rome extended its power all over Italy, by both brute force and alliances.

- **By 264BC,** Rome rivalled Carthage, the North African city that dominated the western Mediterranean. In 164BC, Rome destroyed Carthage totally after the Punic Wars.

- **By 130BC,** Rome had built a mighty empire stretching from Spain to Turkey and along the North African coast.

Rome on the rise

- **As Rome's** empire spread, the creation of plantations worked by slaves put small farmers out of work. The gap between rich and poor widened.

- **Many joined** the army to escape poverty and became more loyal to their generals than to the Senate (the government's ruling body).

- **Two popular generals**, Pompey and Julius Caesar, used their armies to take over Rome and suspend the Republic.

- **Caesar and Pompey** argued, and after battles right across the empire, Caesar gained the upper hand.

- **Once in power,** Caesar restored order and passed laws to reduce people's debts.

- **Caesar was made** dictator and ruled Rome without the Senate.

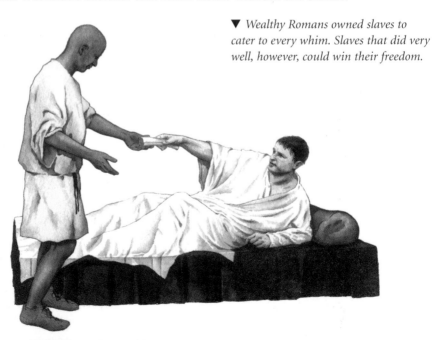

▼ *Wealthy Romans owned slaves to cater to every whim. Slaves that did very well, however, could win their freedom.*

- **In 44BC,** a man called Brutus killed Caesar to restore the Republic – but Caesar's place was taken by another general, Octavian, Caesar's adopted son.

- **By 27BC,** Octavian was so powerful he declared himself the first Roman emperor and took the name Augustus.

- **Under Augustus,** rebellious parts of Spain and the Alps were brought under control and the empire was expanded along the Rhine and Danube Rivers.

- **By 1BC,** the days of strife were over and Rome presided over a vast, stable, prosperous empire.

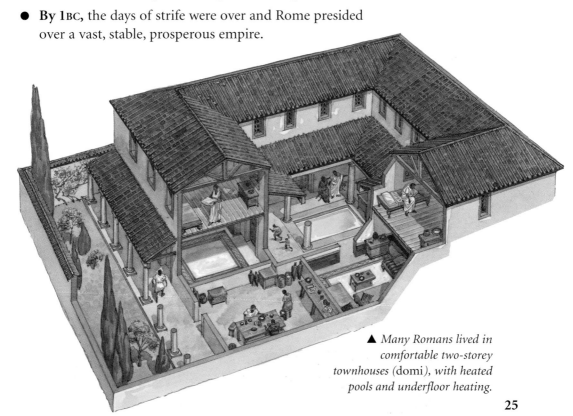

▲ *Many Romans lived in comfortable two-storey townhouses* (domi), *with heated pools and underfloor heating.*

Roman towns

- **Roman towns** were the biggest and most sophisticated the world had seen. They were not built on rigid grids like Greek cities, but they all had common features.

- **Roman towns** had two main streets and many side streets with spaces in between called *insulae* (islands).

▲ *The remains of the forum in Rome give a glimpse of just how magnificent Roman cities must have been.*

- **The insulae** were tightly packed with private houses – houses of the rich, called *domi*, and apartment blocks (also called *insulae*). The bigger Roman houses had courtyards.

- **Traffic jams** were so common that many towns banned wheeled traffic from the streets during daylight.

- **Most towns** had numerous shops, inns (*tabernae*), cafés (*thermopilia*) and bakeries (*pistrina*).

- **The forum** was a large open market and meeting place surrounded on three sides by a covered walkway. On the fourth side was the law courts and the town hall (*basilica*).

- **Most towns** had many grand temples to Roman gods.

- **Most towns** had a large open-air theatre. There was also a games arena, or stadium, where warriors called gladiators fought and chariot races were held.

- **The bath houses** (*thermae*) were places where people came to sit around and dip into hot and cold baths in magnificent surroundings.

- **Towns had** highly sophisticated water supplies and sewage systems.

▼ *The Roman town of Ostia had blocks of flats called 'insulae'. A typical block was three or four storeys high with up to one hundred small, dirty, crowded rooms.*

The Roman Empire

- **For 200 years** after Augustus became emperor in 27BC, Roman emperors ruled over an empire so large and secure that citizens could talk of the Pax Romana (Roman Peace).

- **The Romans built** straight roads to move their troops about quickly. On the whole, they governed peacefully and also built hundreds of towns in the Roman manner.

- **After Augustus** died, in AD14, his stepson Tiberius succeeded him. Then came a succession of Augustus's descendants, including Gaius, Claudius and Nero.

> ...**FASCINATING FACT**...
> Roman historian Suetonius claimed that
> Nero sang and played the lyre during
> Rome's great fire in AD64.

- **Gaius** (AD37–41) was known as Caligula ('little boots') because of the soldiers' boots he wore as a child.

- **Soon after** Caligula became emperor, an illness left him mad. He spent wildly, had people whipped and killed, married and murdered his sister and elected his horse as a minister. Eventually he was murdered by soldiers.

- **Claudius** (AD41–54) replaced Caligula. People thought he was stupid because he stuttered and was physically disabled. However, he proved the wisest and most humane of all emperors.

◀ *Gladiators were prisoners and criminals who were made to fight in big arenas called amphitheatres to entertain people.*

▶ *The orange area of this map shows the empire at its peak under the Emperor Trajan (AD98–117). It was divided into areas called provinces, such as Britannia (England and Wales) and Gallia (northern France). Each had its own Roman governor, often a retired consul (minister), who used his power to extort taxes.*

▼ *Leading imperial officials wore distinctive flowing robes called togas. Laws were written on papyrus or parchment.*

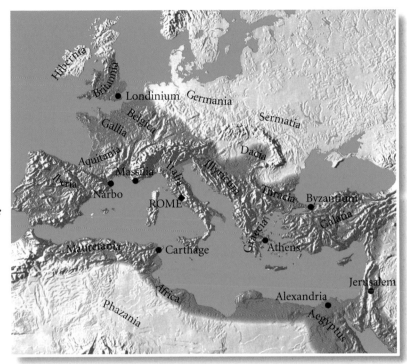

- **Claudius** was probably poisoned by his fourth wife Agrippina, who wanted power for her son Nero.

- **The power** of Roman emperors reached a peak under the 'Antonines' – Nerva, Trajan, Hadrian, Antoninus and Marcus Aurelius. They ruled AD96–180.

- **The Roman** empire grew only a little after Augustus's death. Britain was conquered in AD43, and Emperor Trajan took Dacia (now Hungary and Romania).

29

Roman Britain

- **The Roman** occupation began in earnest when the armies of Claudius landed at Richborough in Kent in AD43. All of England and Wales was conquered by AD78.

- **Scotland remained** beyond Roman control. In AD122–130, the 118-km-long stone wall that is now called Hadrian's wall was built right across the country to act as a frontier.

- **The Roman army** in Britain was powerful. There were three legions (5000 men each) at York, Chester and Caerleon, plus 40,000 auxiliaries.

- **Roman Britain** was ruled by a Roman governor, but the Romans co-opted local chiefs to help.

- **The Romans built** the first proper towns in Britain – like St Albans, Gloucester and Lincoln – with typical Roman features such as baths and theatres.

- **Demand for food** and leather from the army and the new towns boosted farming. Large estates centred on Roman-style villas grew rich, but even small farmers did well.

- **Most people** were bilingual, speaking both Celtic and Latin, and many adopted Roman lifestyles.

▶ *King Arthur became the greatest hero in British legend, but the real Arthur was probably a British chief who, for a while, turned the tide against the Anglo-Saxons with a victory at Mt Badon around AD530–550.*

30

- **When barbarians** attacked the empire on the continent in the AD300s, leading generals from Italy were sent to reorganise defences. Power fell into the hands of tyrants like the British king Vortigern (AD425–250).

- **Vortigern invited** Anglo-Saxons from Germany to settle in the east to help him against rebel Britons. But the Anglo-Saxons soon turned against him and invited in others of their kind to join them.

- **Villas and towns** were abandoned and Britons fled west or abroad as the Anglo-Saxons moved in.

▲ *Hadrian's wall may have acted as a defence, keeping 'barbarians' out of Roman territory. It is generally accepted that the emperor Hadrian wanted to mark the northern boundary of his empire. The wall itself took six years to build, and was modified for many years after.*

31

The Roman army

- **Rome owed** its power to its highly efficient army.

- **In a crisis,** Rome could raise an army of 800,000 men.

- **The Roman army** fought mainly on foot, advancing in tight squares bristling with spears and protected by large shields called *scutari*. They often put shields over their heads to protect them from arrows. This formation was called a *testudo* – or 'tortoise'.

- **Under the Republic,** the army was divided into legions of 5000 soldiers. Legions were made up of 10 cohorts. Cohorts, in turn, consisted of centuries containing 80–100 soldiers.

- **Each legion** was led by a *legatus*. A cohort was led by a *tribunus militum*. A century was led by a *centurion*.

- **All Roman soldiers** had a short sword (60 cm long) and carried two throwing spears. They also wore armour – first, vests of chain mail and a leather helmet; later, metal strips on a leather tunic and a metal helmet.

- **Roman armies** built huge siege engines and catapults when they had to capture a town.

- **After 100BC,** most Roman soldiers were professionals, who joined the army for life. Food accounted for about a third of their wages.

- **In training,** soldiers went on forced 30-km marches three times a month. They moved at 8 km per hour, carrying very heavy packs.

- **Soldiers were flogged** for misbehaviour. Mutiny was punished by executing one in ten suspects. This was called *decimation*.

◄ The testudo *formation proved itself highly effective for Roman foot-soldiers.*

▶ Roman soldiers had to be tough – while on the march they carried all their weapons and armour, plus a pack full of clothes, food and tools for digging and building.

How Romans lived

- **In big cities,** rich Romans had a comfortable way of life.

- **For breakfast,** Romans typically ate bread or wheat biscuits with honey, dates or olives, and water or wine.

- **A Roman lunch** (*prandium*) consisted of much the same things as breakfast.

- **Romans had cena** (the main meal) in the afternoon, typically after a visit to the baths. This became a very lavish affair with three main courses, and each course had many dishes.

- **Rich Romans** had a lot of free time, since slaves did all the work. Leisure activities included gambling by tossing coins (*capita et navia*) and knucklebones (*tali*).

- **Public entertainments** were called *ludi* (games). They included theatre, chariot races, and fights with gladiators (trained fighters) and animals.

- **The Emperor** Trajan went to a gladiator contest that lasted 117 days and involved 10,000 gladiators.

- **Romans** had more slaves than any empire in history. Many were treated cruelly, but some lived quite well.

- **Between 73–71BC,** a man called Spartacus led a revolt of slaves that lasted two years, until it was crushed by Roman armies.

▶ *Romans were very clean and spent many hours at public baths or bathing at home. These are the Roman baths at Bath, England.*

Julius Caesar

- **Julius Caesar** (*c.*100–44BC) was Rome's most famous general and leader. He was also a great speaker who had the power to excite huge crowds.

- **Caesar's** individuality was clear from the start. At 17, he defied Sulla, the dictator of Rome and married Cornelia, the daughter of the rebel leader Cinna. Cornelia died when Caesar was about 30.

- **Caesar began** as a politician and made himself popular by spending his own money on public entertainments.

- **In 60BC,** he formed a powerful triumvirate (group of three people) with Crassus and Pompey, which dominated Rome.

- **In 58BC,** Caesar led a brilliantly organized campaign to conquer Gaul (now northern France), and also invaded Britain.

  - **Caesar** wrote an account of his campaigns in Gaul that is a classic of historical writing.

  - **Pompey** was alarmed by the fame that Caesar's conquests brought him. The two began a war that lasted five years, ending in Egypt in 48BC, where Caesar met and fell in love with Cleopatra.

  - **By 45BC,** Caesar was undisputed master of the Roman Empire. The people elected him dictator for life.

▲ *Caesar was not only a brilliant general, but a great statesman who brought in many reforms and tried to stamp out corruption.*

- **Caesar was asked** to become king, but he refused.

- **On March 15,** 44BC – called 'the Ides of March' – Caesar was stabbed to death as he entered the Senate. His assassins were a group led by Brutus and Cassius, who felt that his ambitions were a threat to Rome.

▶ *Caesar planned all kinds of bold economic, social and government reforms – but had been unable to carry many of them out by the time he was assassinated.*

37

The fall of Rome

- **After the death** of Marcus Aurelius, in AD180, Rome was plagued by various serious political struggles.

- **The Praetorian Guard** (the emperor's personal soldiers) chose or deposed emperors at will, and there were 60 emperors between AD235 and 284 alone.

- **The Empire fell** into anarchy and was beset by famine, plague and invasion.

▼ *After the emperor Constantine moved his capital there in AD330, Byzantium (now Istanbul in Turkey) became the main defender of Roman civilization.*

- **Diocletian** (emperor from AD284) tried to make the empire easier to govern by splitting it in two halves – East and West. He asked Maximian to rule the west.

- **Diocletian retired** 'to grow cabbages' at his palace in Dalmatia, and soldiers tried to choose a new emperor.

- **Constantine,** commander of the Roman armies in Britain, defeated his rivals to become emperor. It is said that before the main battle, he saw a Christian cross in the sky. After his victory, he became Christian.

- **In BC330,** Constantine made Byzantium (now Istanbul) his capital and called it Constantinople.

- **After Constantine's death,** the empire fell into chaos again. It became split permanently into East and West.

- **The Western empire** suffered attacks from barbarians. Vandals invaded Spain and North Africa. Goths and Huns such as Attila attacked from the North.

- **In AD410,** Visigoths led by Alaric invaded Italy and sacked (burned and looted) Rome. In AD455, Vandals sacked Rome again. In AD476, the Western empire finally collapsed.

▶ *This coin was minted during the reign of Constantine. The inscription translates as 'Constantine, dutiful and wise ruler'.*

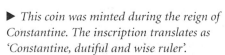

39

Index